# AMAZING ORiGAMi

# Origami
# Games

Joe Fullman

Gareth Stevens
PUBLISHING

**Please visit our website, www.garethstevens.com. For a free color catalog of all our high-quality books, call toll free 1-800-542-2595 or fax 1-877-542-2596.**

Cataloging-in-Publication Data
Fullman, Joe.
Origami games / by Joe Fullman.
p. cm. — (Amazing origami)
Includes index.
ISBN 978-1-4824-4159-8 (pbk.)
ISBN 978-1-4824-4160-4 (6-pack)
ISBN 978-1-4824-4161-1 (library binding)
1. Origami — Juvenile literature. 2. Games — Juvenile literature.
I. Fullman, Joe. II. Title.
TT870.F85 2016
736'.982—d23

First Edition

Published in 2016 by
**Gareth Stevens Publishing**
111 East 14ᵗʰ Street, Suite 349
New York, NY 10003

Copyright © 2016 Arcturus Publishing

Models and photography: Belinda Webster and Michael Wiles
Text: Joe Fullman
Design: Emma Randall
Editor: Frances Evans

Printed in the United States of America
CPSIA compliance information: Batch CW16GS: For further information contact Gareth Stevens, New York, New York at 1-800-542-2595.

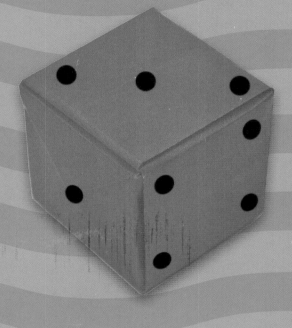

# Contents

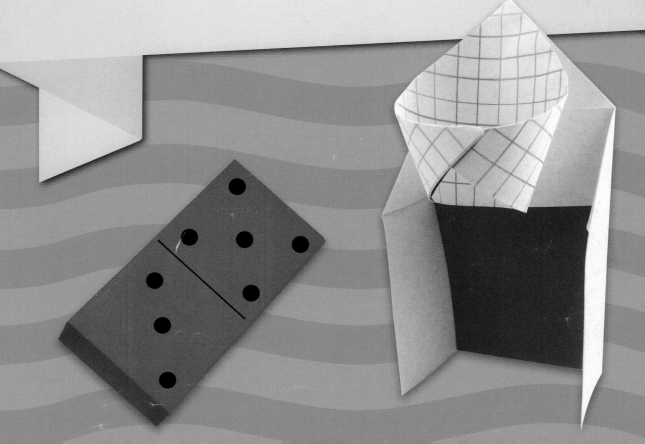

# Basic Folds

**Origami has been popular in Japan for hundreds of years and is now loved all around the world. You can make great models with just one sheet of paper... and this book shows you how!**

The paper used in origami is thin but strong, so that it can be folded many times. It is usually colored on one side. Alternatively you can use ordinary scrap paper, but make sure it's not too thick.

Origami models often share the same folds and basic designs. This introduction explains some of the folds that you will need for the projects in this book, and they will also come in useful if you make other origami models. When making the models in this book, follow the key below to find out what the lines and arrows mean. And always crease well!

## KEY

valley fold ‑ ‑ ‑ ‑ ‑ ‑ ‑ ‑ ‑ ‑ ‑

mountain fold ....................

step fold (mountain and valley fold next to each other)

direction to move paper

push ◄

## MOUNTAIN FOLD

*To make a mountain fold, fold the paper so that the crease is pointing up towards you, like a mountain.*

## VALLEY FOLD

*To make a valley fold, fold the paper the other way, so that the crease is pointing away from you, like a valley.*

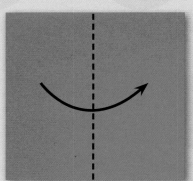

## A NOTE ABOUT MEASUREMENTS

Measurements are given in U.S. form with the metric in parentheses. The metric conversion is rounded to make it easier to measure.

# INSIDE REVERSE FOLD

An inside reverse fold is useful if you want to make a nose or a tail, or if you want to flatten off the shape of another part of an origami model.

**1** Practice by first folding a piece of paper diagonally in half. Make a valley fold on one point and crease.

**2** It's important to make sure that the paper is creased well. Run your finger over the crease two or three times.

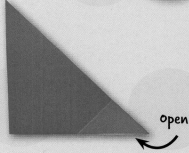
open

**3** Unfold and open up the corner slightly. Refold the crease nearest to you into a mountain fold.

**4** Open up the paper a little more and then tuck the tip of the point inside. Close the paper. This is the view from the underside of the paper.

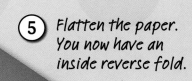

**5** Flatten the paper. You now have an inside reverse fold.

# OUTSIDE REVERSE FOLD

An outside reverse fold is useful if you want to make a head, beak or foot, or another part of your model that sticks out.

**1** Practice by first folding a piece of paper diagonally in half. Make a valley fold on one point and crease.

**2** It's important to make sure that the paper is creased well. Run your finger over the crease two or three times.

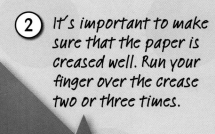

**3** Unfold and open up the corner slightly. Refold the crease furthest away from you into a valley fold.

open

**4** Open up the paper a little more and start to turn the corner inside out. Then close the paper when the fold begins to turn.

**5** You now have an outside reverse fold. You can either flatten the paper or leave it rounded out.

# Dominoes

It's great fun to send a row of dominoes toppling over. Try making a few of these in different colors, carefully line them up and then watch them fall!

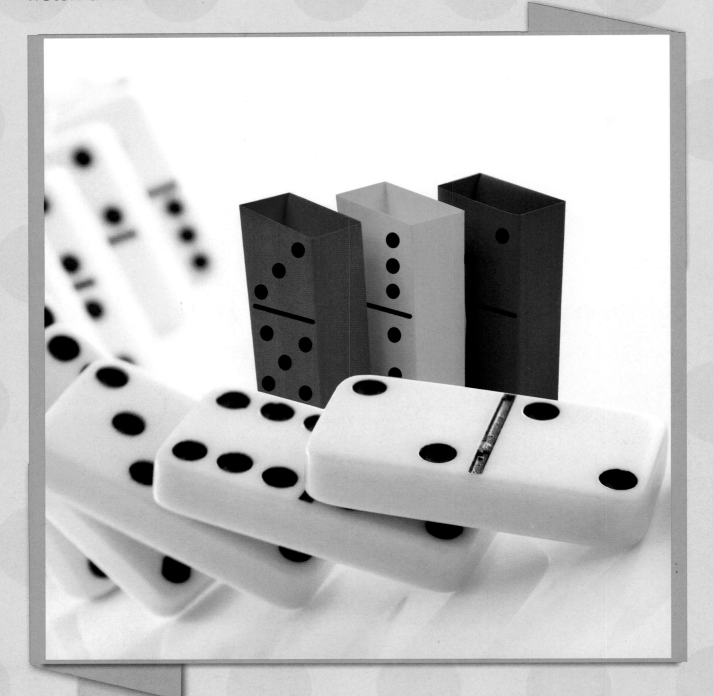

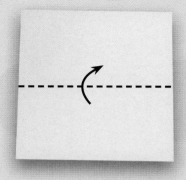

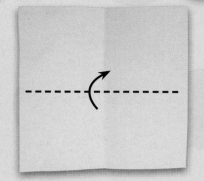

1. Start with the paper white side up and a straight edge facing you. Valley fold the bottom edge up to the top, but don't crease.

2. Make a small crease on the left edge, then unfold.

3. Turn the paper 90° clockwise so the small crease is at the top. Valley fold the bottom edge up to the top, but again don't crease.

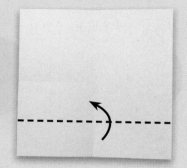

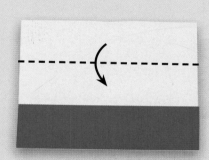

4. Again, make a small crease on the left edge.

5. Unfold and then valley fold the bottom edge to the center (marked by the small crease).

6. This time make a hard crease all the way along the fold. Then fold the top half down to the center.

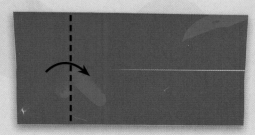

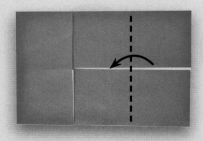

7. There should be slightly more white showing on the right than on the left. Fold the left edge to the crease mark in the middle.

8. Fold the right edge all the way to the left edge.

(9) Your paper should look this. Unfold the right flap.

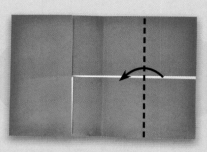

(10) Fold the right edge over so it meets the edge of the left flap.

(11) Your paper should now look like this. Unfold the left flap.

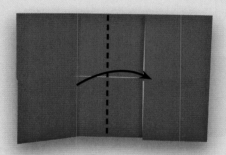

(12) Fold the left edge all the way to the right edge.

(13) Your paper should look like this, with a vertical crease about a quarter of the way from the left edge, and a small horizontal crease on the right edge.

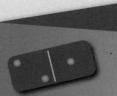

## Did You Know?

The most dominoes toppled in a single attempt was more than 4.5 million in 2009 in the Netherlands. It took weeks to set all the dominoes up – and several hours to knock them all down again!

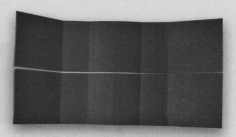

**14** Completely unfold the two flaps, so your paper looks like this.

**15** Curl the paper over and insert the left flap (the one with the crease mark) inside the right-hand flap (the one without a crease mark).

**16** Keep pushing the left flap inside the other flap.

**17** Once it's all the way inside, your domino is ready.

**18** Make a set of dominoes using different colors!

# Fortune Teller

This playground favorite is easy to make and even easier to use. Try it on your friends – but be sure to think up some fun fortunes for them first!

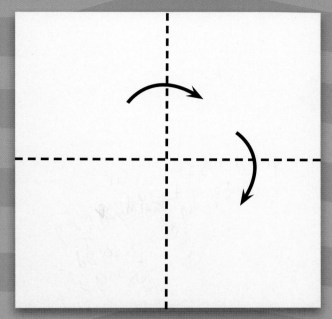

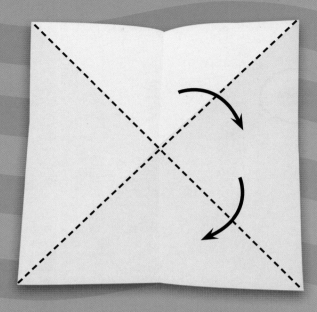

① Place your paper white side up. Valley fold from top to bottom and unfold. Then valley fold from left to right and unfold.

② Now, still with the paper white side up, valley fold the paper diagonally one way and unfold. Then do the same on the other side.

③ Fold the top left corner diagonally to the middle point.

④ Repeat step 3 with the other three corners.

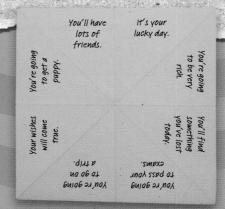

**5** Turn the paper over from left to right.

**6** Now your need to write a fortune into each of the eight small triangles made by the folds.

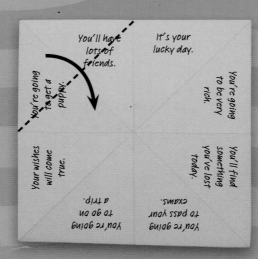

**7** Fold the top left corner diagonally to the middle point.

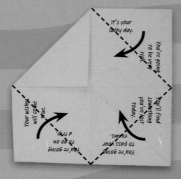

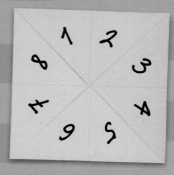

**8** Repeat step 7 with the other three corners, then turn the paper over.

**9** Write the numbers 1 to 8 in each of the small triangles.

**10** Turn the paper over.
Add a color to each
of the four squares.

**11** Use the thumb and first finger
of each hand to push open
your fortune teller.

**12** Turn the model over and your
fortune teller is ready to tell
its first fortune.

## How to Use Your Fortune Teller

Place the first finger and thumb of both
hands inside the teller. Get a friend to pick
a color. Spell out the color, such as
G-R-E-E-N, moving your fingers in and
out with each letter. Show your friend the
inside of the fortune teller and get them
to choose one of the numbers they can
see. Count off the number, again moving
your fingers in and out with each digit.
Show your friend the inside of the teller
once more and get them to pick a number.
Open it up and read them their fortune!

# Basketball Hoop

Invite your friends over for a game of origami basketball using this great hoop and a scrunched up piece of paper as a ball! You'll need a pencil to draw the net.

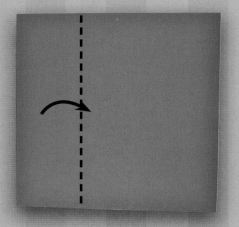

1. Place your paper as shown and make a valley fold a third of the way from the left edge.

2. Valley fold the right edge over to the left edge.

3. Your paper should look like this.

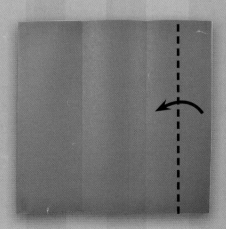

4. Unfold the paper and fold the right edge so it meets the right-hand crease.

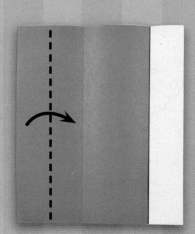

5. Fold the left edge so it meets the left-hand crease.

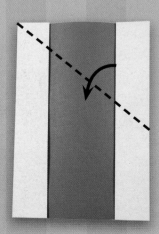

6. Diagonally fold the top right-hand corner down to the left edge.

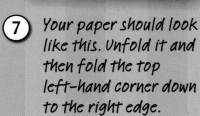

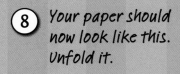

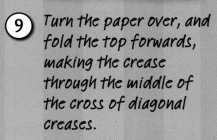

**7** Your paper should look like this. Unfold it and then fold the top left-hand corner down to the right edge.

**8** Your paper should now look like this. Unfold it.

**9** Turn the paper over, and fold the top forwards, making the crease through the middle of the cross of diagonal creases.

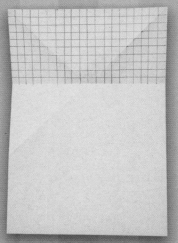

**10** Unfold the paper.

**11** Use your pencil to draw a net pattern in the area above the horizontal crease.

**12** Turn the paper over so it looks like this.

## Did You Know?

The first game of basketball was played in 1891 using a basket for carrying peaches. Today's metal baskets have a 18-inch (45 cm) diameter and are set exactly 10 feet (3 m) off the ground.

 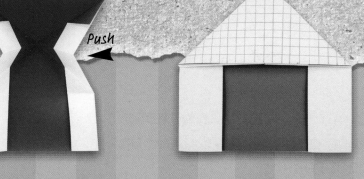 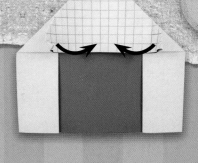

**13** Start pushing the two sides of the horizontal crease together, like this.

**14** Keep pushing until a triangle shape forms. Flatten it down.

**15** Start curling the ends of the triangle towards each other.

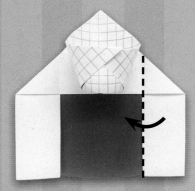 

**16** Keep curling until the two ends meet, then tuck one end inside the other to hold the basket in place. Fold the right-hand side to the center.

**17** Fold the left-hand side to the center.

 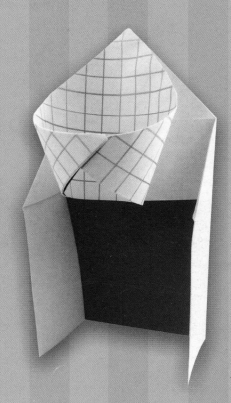

**18** Your paper should look like this.

**19** Open the last two folds up, so the flaps stick out. Now stand your basket up and shoot some hoops!

# Dice

Dice are used in lots of different games. Follow these instructions to make some dice of your own, draw on the dots with a felt-tip pen, and then get rolling!

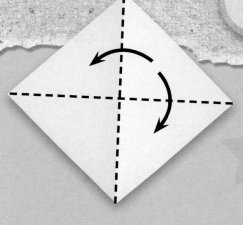

① You'll need two pieces of paper for this project, which you'll need to fold in exactly the same way.

② Place the first piece of paper like this. Valley fold in half from left to right, and unfold. Then valley fold in half from top to bottom, and unfold.

③ Take the left point and fold it over to meet the center line.

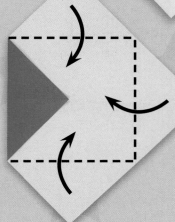

④ Repeat step 3 with the other three points.

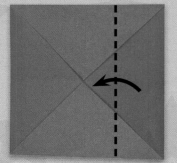

⑤ Make a vertical valley fold a third of the way from the right side.

(6) Fold the left edge all the way over to the right edge to form a tube shape.

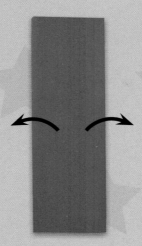

(7) Unfold the folds you made in steps 5 and 6.

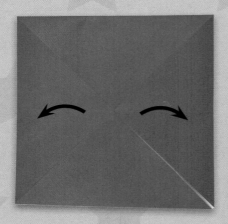

(8) Unfold the left and right sides.

(9) Your paper should look like this. Make a valley fold a third of the way from the top edge.

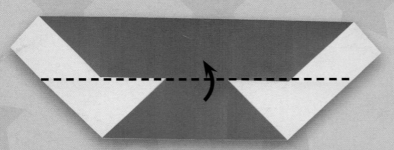

(10) Valley fold the bottom edge to the top to make a long thin shape.

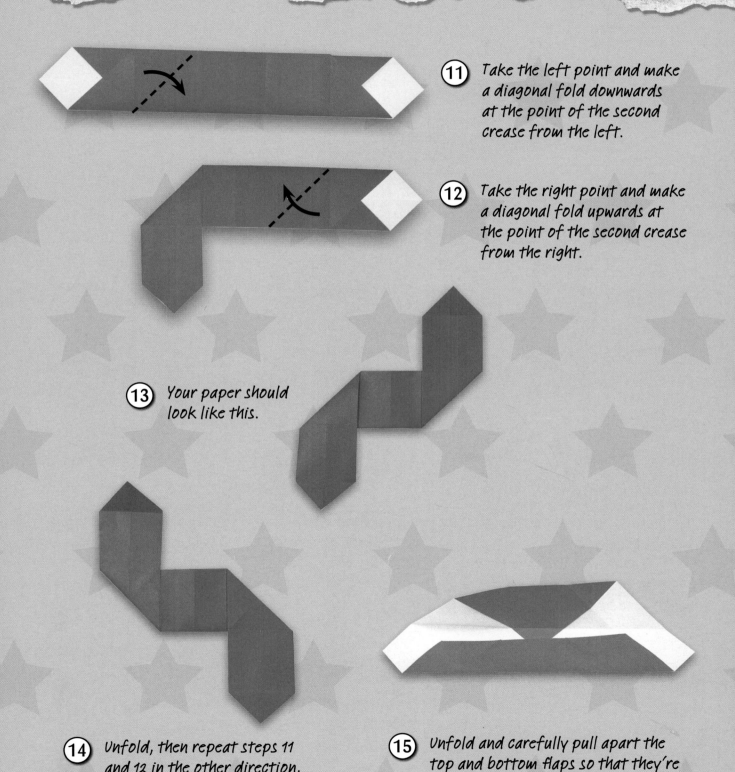

11. Take the left point and make a diagonal fold downwards at the point of the second crease from the left.

12. Take the right point and make a diagonal fold upwards at the point of the second crease from the right.

13. Your paper should look like this.

14. Unfold, then repeat steps 11 and 12 in the other direction, so your paper looks like this.

15. Unfold and carefully pull apart the top and bottom flaps so that they're parallel to each other, like this.

**16** Start to gently push the folds on the left-hand side towards you.

*Push*

*Push*

**17** Turn the paper around so the open side is facing you. Tuck the far side over to form one side of the cube.

**18** Now start pushing the folds together on the other side.

**19** Turn the paper around again, and tuck the point over to complete your model.

## Did You Know?

The first dice were invented in the Middle East more than 5,000 years ago and were made of animal bone. They were originally used for trying to predict the future rather than playing games.

20 The first half of your dice is now complete.

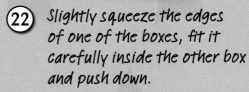

21 Use the other sheet of paper and repeat steps 1 to 19 to make the other half of the dice.

22 Slightly squeeze the edges of one of the boxes, fit it carefully inside the other box and push down.

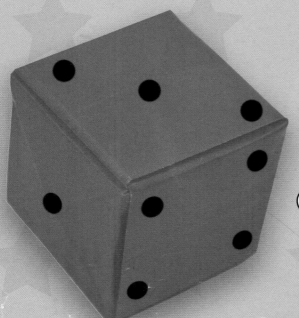

23 Once the two boxes have been fitted together, use a felt-tip pen to draw on some dots. Then it's ready to roll!

# Spinning Top

This multicolored top really does spin! It takes a little while to make, but it's guaranteed to provide hours of spinning fun.

1. To make the spinning top, you need three sheets of different colored paper.

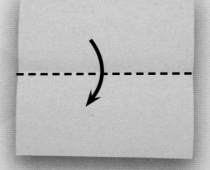

2. Place your first sheet of paper white side up. Valley fold it from top to bottom, then unfold.

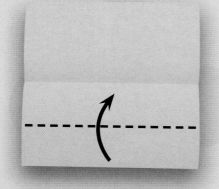

3. Valley fold the bottom edge up to the center line.

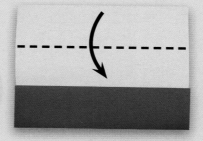

4. Valley fold the top edge to the center line.

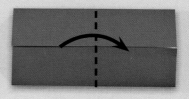

5. Valley fold the paper in half from left to right, then unfold.

6. Valley fold the left-hand edge to the center line.

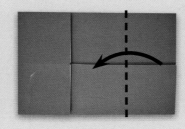

7. Valley fold the right-hand edge to meet the left flap.

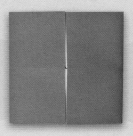

8. Your paper should look like this.

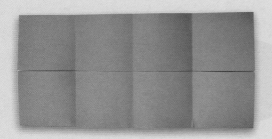

**9** Unfold steps 6 and 7.

**10** Push up the left-hand edge so it's vertical. Then make a diagonal fold in one of the small squares in the bottom left, like this.

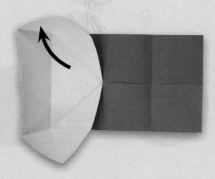

**11** Repeat step 10 in the left-hand top half.

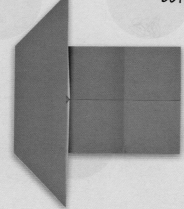

**12** Press down the left-hand side to make this shape.

**13** Repeat steps 10, 11 and 12 on the right-hand side, so your paper looks like this. Take the top left-hand point and diagonally fold it to the left.

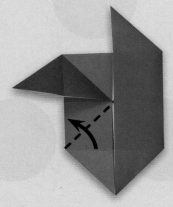

**14** Take the bottom left-hand point and diagonally fold it to the left.

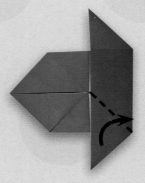

**15** Take the bottom right-hand point and fold it diagonally to the right.

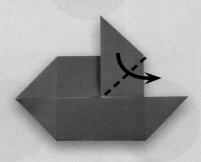

**16** Take the top right-hand point and fold it diagonally to the right.

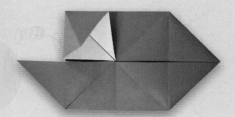

17 Your paper should now look like this.

18 Lift up the top left-hand corner and open it out, so it looks like a bird's mouth.

19 Flatten the paper down to form a square, like this.

20 Repeat steps 18 and 19 with the three other points. This will leave you with four mini squares. In the top left square, valley fold the bottom edge up to meet the diagonal center line.

21 Now fold the top edge of the top left mini square to meet the diagonal center line.

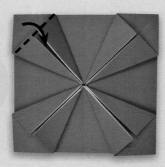

22 Repeat steps 20 and 21 with the other 3 mini squares.

23 Fold over the top left corner of the top left mini square.

24 Repeat step 23 for the other three corners.

(25) Your paper should now look like this.

(26) In the top left-hand corner, open up the three folds you just made.

(27) Lift up the point at the center so it forms a shape a bit like a bird's mouth.

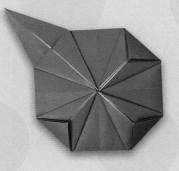

(28) Flatten the paper down, leaving you with this pointed shape.

(29) Repeat steps 26, 27 and 28 for the other three corners. Your paper should look like this.

(30) On the right-hand side, take the center point and fold it to the right, like this. Then repeat the step with the other three center points.

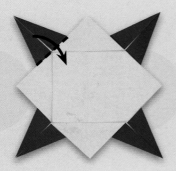

(31) Fold the top left point in towards the center.

(32) Repeat step 31 with the other 3 corners.

(33) Your first model piece is ready.

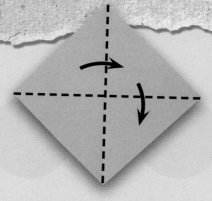

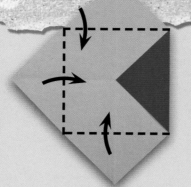

**1** With your paper white side up and pointing towards you, make two diagonal valley folds, then unfold.

**2** Fold the right-hand corner to the middle point. Then do the same with the other 3 corners.

**3** Your paper should look like this.

**4** Turn the paper over. Fold the top right-hand corner to the middle point. Then do the same with the other three corners.

**5** Your paper should look like this.

**6** Turn the paper over again, and fold the top right-hand corner to the middle point. Then do the same with the other three corners.

**7** Your paper should look like this.

**8** Turn the paper over again and fold out the top right flap from the middle point. Then do the same with the other three flaps.

**9** Your second model piece is now ready. Put it to one side and pick up your third piece of paper.

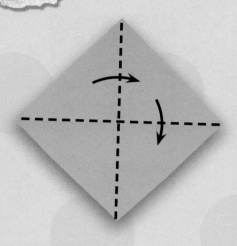

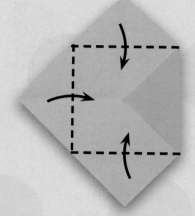

1. Place your paper white side up. Make two diagonal valley folds, then unfold.

2. Fold the top right corner to the middle point. Then do the same with the other three corners.

3. Your paper should look like this. Take the top right corner and fold it to the middle point.

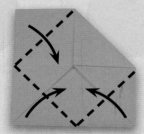

4. Fold the other three corners to the middle.

5. Again, fold the top right-hand corner to the middle.

6. Then fold the other three corners to the middle.

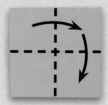

7. Your paper should look like this.

8. Turn the paper over and make two valley folds along the vertical and horizontal lines.

9. Now, push in the folds made along the vertical and horizontal lines to form a star shape, like this.

① Take Model Piece 2 and insert the top left corner into Model Piece 1, like this.

② Repeat with the other 3 corners.

③ Now take Model Piece 3 and insert the legs under the flaps of Model Piece 2, like this.

④ Once all four legs are in position and secure, your super spinning top is ready. Give it a spin!

# Glossary

**basketball** A game played between two teams of five players, in which points are scored by throwing a ball through a hoop at each end of the court.

**crease** A line in a piece of paper made by folding.

**diameter** A straight line passing through the center of something, especially a circle or sphere.

**fortune** What is going to happen to someone in the future.

**mountain fold** An origami step where a piece of paper is folded so that the crease is pointing upwards, like a mountain.

**parallel** To be side by side with something.

**secure** Fixed so as not to become loose, give way or be lost.

**step fold** A mountain fold and valley fold next to each other.

**topple** To cause something to become unsteady and fall over.

**valley fold** An origami step where a piece of paper is folded so that the crease is pointing downwards, like a valley.

# Further Reading

Akass, Susan. *My First Origami Book*. Cico Kidz, 2011.

Heiman, Diana and Suneby, Liz. *Origami Fortune Tellers*. Dover Publications Inc., 2011.

Robinson, Nick. *The Awesome Origami Pack*. Barron's Educational Series, Inc., 2014.

# Index